SPECTACULAR SWEDEN

SCENES OF SURPRISE AND WONDER

ANITA SHENOI

Thank you Karen for
being the opponent for
my dissertation.
With hopes to meet you
again.
Best / Karine Ingelbked

Kakao förlag
Box 1505
221 01 Lund
Sweden
www.kakao.se

Text: Anita Shenoi

Printed in Estonia 2016 via Italgraf Media
ISBN: 9789187795206

SPECTACULAR SWEDEN

SCENES OF SURPRISE AND WONDER

ANITA SHENOI

CONTENTS

A WALK ON THE WILD SIDE

RAPADALEN, SAREK

Rapaätno, Tjaktjajaure, Kvikkjokk. Names as exotic-sounding and enticing as the places they refer to. In the most remote wilderness area of Europe there are no roads or trails, no shelters from the rain, no bridges to ease your crossing of forcefully flowing rivers. No mobile phone signal. Just the prospect of 9 400 km² of deep cut valleys and jagged peaks.

Silence. Or did you hear a rustle in the bushes? If it is September, you could be in for a shock as a giant moose calmly trots past you, following the scent of a future mate. This is the home of The Wild: the bear, the wolverine, the lynx, the golden eagle... A foreign territory in which to tread carefully. Enter at your own risk, for a true adventure!

Sarek goes with... National Park, UNESCO World Heritage Site, Kungsleden hiking trail, outdoor adventure

DOGGED DETERMINATION

LAPLAND

They've got beauty, brains and are born to run – who better to transport you over the icy wilderness than an eager team of Huskies? Nothing beats the feeling of all that raw energy at the reins, powder whipping up into your face and evaporating in the surprising warmth of the winter sun.

But after roaming the never-ending white expanse for a while, the thought of sipping a whiskey in front of a roaring fire becomes increasingly appealing. And what do you know – there, on the horizon, a reindeer herder on his scooter, ready to guide you back to civilisation!

Fun fact: Huskies are known for their incredible pulling strength – up to ten times their own weight or more. Recent IWPA championships have recorded Alaskan Malamutes pulling over 900 kg!

AIN'T NO MOUNTAIN HIGH ENOUGH

NALLO

The vast stone fields surrounding the base of Nallo mountain can be tricky terrain for tired hikers seeking refuge at the small mountain station. The lake provides crystal clear water for your kettle though, so after a hot meal and a good night's rest you can wake up to a beautiful new day of challenges – perhaps climbing to the top of Nallo to see all the way to Kebnekaise, Sweden's highest mountain.

Did you know? STF (the Swedish Tourist Association) has numerous mountain huts and stations along hiking or ski trails where you can enjoy basic accommodation and maybe a well-earned sauna.

I CAN SEE CLEARLY NOW

KÄRKEVAGGE VALLEY

Aquafina, Evian, Fiji – watch out – at Kärkevagge, 15 km east of the Norwegian border, you'll find a strong contender for the purest water. Deep in the valley is Lake Rissajaure, famed for the exceptional purity and clarity of its glacial melt water. The lake is so clear, you can see right to the bottom, 36 metres down.

Did you know? In the Sami language, Rissajaure means 'the lake that flashes like fire'.

17

THERE'S SOMETHING OUT THERE...

LAPLAND

Has a UFO landed? When the night sky goes fluorescent green we can only wonder. Scientists say it's all about the collision of charged particles with atoms in the high-altitude atmosphere. So as spooky and unreal as it may seem, the Aurora Borealis is a most natural phenomenon.

This swirling, glowing theatrical in the sky is most likely to be seen on a cold winter's evening in the north of Sweden, where the clear, unpolluted atmosphere guarantees a front row experience.

Lapland goes with... Spaceport Sweden, dog sledging, Ice hotel, Europe's last wilderness

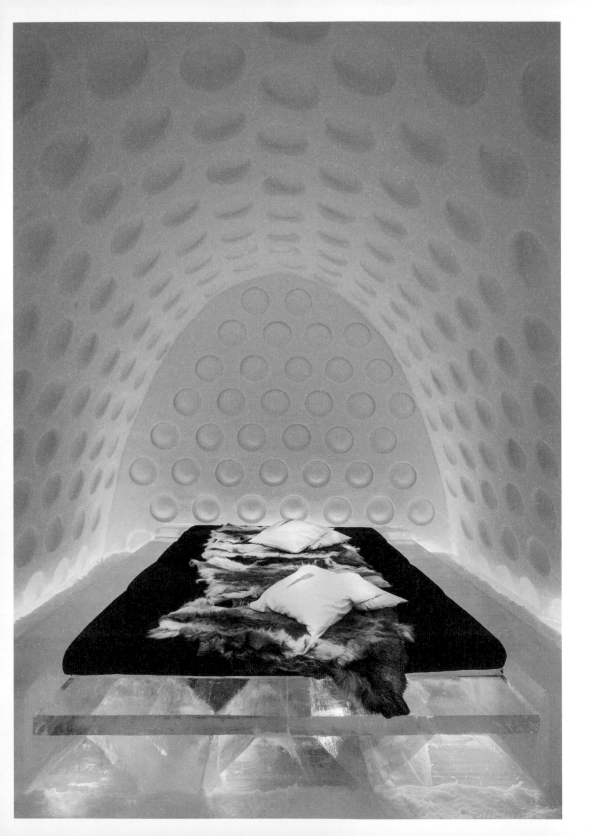

COOL PYJAMAS

ICEHOTEL, JUKKASJÄRVI

A drip of water is often casually dismissed but dangle an icicle in front of us and suddenly, we're mesmerised. It is this fascination with the properties of crystalline H_2O that has inspired the intricate art of ice sculpture, and it is here at Jukkasjärvi, on the mighty river Torne, that it has resulted in the now world famous and unique ice art experience: The Icehotel.

Do you dare to spend a night in the cold? Luckily, the hotel provides expedition-style sleeping bags and ample reindeer skins, so you can enjoy the cool blue of your room without going blue in the face.

Did you know? The Icehotel is the ultimate in recycling. Each spring, blocks of ice are harvested from the river and stored, ready to build with the following winter. Each summer, the hotel melts and the water returns to its source.

BEETLE MANIA

SKATAN ECOPARK, VINDELN

A comfortable carpet of moss and lichen tempts you to set up camp. As you settle down and darkness falls, are you as snug as a bug in a rug? A scratching sound here, a little scurrying there – perhaps you're not the only one who loves Skatan…

Because this is beetle country! Sparse pine forests and a unique rolling landscape formed by ancient inland ice melt makes Skatan the perfect habitat for all kinds of bug, from the more familiar Longhorn (Tragosoma depsarium) to the extremely rare and tiny water beetle (Ochtebius nilssoni).

Did you know? The Vindel river region is applying to become a UNESCO biosphere reserve by demonstrating its ability to encourage sustainable development along with preservation of ecosystems and biodiversity.

RIVER RAPIDS RUN DEEP

VINDEL RIVER

The many waterways running through Västerbotten make it a kayaking wonderland. For the adrenaline junkie, rafting on the rapids of the Vindel river is not to be missed!

YABBA-DABBA DOO

NÄMFORSEN

Feeling as intrepid as a Stone Age hunter? You can follow their tracks at Nämforsen, Näsåker, the site of one of the largest collections of rock carvings in Europe. Along the shores of these rapids there are some 2 600 different figures chipped into the rock, the oldest of which are believed to date from around 4 500 BC.

Fun fact: During the first weekend of August each year, the tiny village of Näsåker attracts thousands of visitors as it hosts the hippy-style world music festival Urkult.

TAKE ME HIGHER

HÖGA KUSTEN

Of Sweden's 11 500 kilometres of mainland coast, only the stretch between Härnösand and Örnsköldsvik merits the title Höga kusten or The High Coast. Post-glacial rebound has caused the land in this area to rise 800 metres, creating a dramatic landscape with high cliffs.

The scenery is best surveyed from the top of Skuleberget, a mountain towering 294 metres over the sea and equipped with Europe's largest *via ferrata*, making the climb up less of a cliff hanger.

Did you know? Höga Kusten is also the home of *surströmming*. The stinky fermented Baltic herring has been a staple in the north of Sweden for centuries but is often regarded as an oddity by outsiders, who may lack the courage to try it!

PHOENIX FROM THE FLAMES

SUNDSVALL

Swedish timber burns bright – a blessing and a curse that the sawmill heartlands of Sweden have learnt to live with through the ages. Up and down the coast of Norrland, towns were either being burnt to the ground by foreign plunderers or ignited by some freakish accident – as was the case in 1888, when it is said a spark from a steamship sent Sundsvall up in smoke.

Sensibly, the centre of Sundsvall was rebuilt in stone, and it could resume its rise as a major industrial centre. Today, the city remains an important hub for Västernorrland and now boasts a graceful new bridge, easing traffic along the logistical lifeline of the E4.

SLIPPERY SLOPE TO SUCCESS

ÅRE

Åre has come a long way since its early days as a minor tourist destination in the late 19th Century, when the new railroad made it possible for 'air guests' to go and climb Åreskutan mountain and enjoy some fresh O_2.

With the addition of the Åre Bergbana cable car and a handful of hotels, Åre's future as a tourist attraction was secured, and now the area has developed into a thriving ski resort and hosted major international competitions, such as the 2007 Alpine World Championships.

Looking down over the valley from the slopes is always a pleasure – which is your favourite part of the system – Åre Village, Duved or Åre Björnen?

A RUSH OF BLOOD TO THE HEAD

TÄNNFORSEN

Feel the power, as the din and crashing roar of the cascade fills your ears! Tännforsen, northwest of Åre, is Sweden's largest waterfall, gushing as much as 740 cubic metres per second at its peak volume in the spring. In winter, things are a little slower, as the crisp cold air freezes large parts of the water fall, creating beautiful ice formations.

NO DOUBT ABOUT IT

MORA

Sweden might not have been Swedish had it not been for two men from Mora. In 1520, Gustav Vasa was busy rallying support around the country for a rebellion against the occupying Danes.

Legend has it that the townspeople of Mora were unconvinced at first but later changed their minds, sending their two fastest skiers to catch up with Vasa in Sälen. With that pivotal turn of support, Vasa went on to become the most famous king of Sweden and the rest, of course, is history!

Mora goes with… Vasaloppet, Mora knife, Dala horse, Anders Zorn, Kurbits, Faluröd

METEORITIC ACOUSTICS

DALHALLA, RÄTTVIK

Neil Young, ZZ Top, Pink Floyd… just a few of the world famous musical acts that have performed at Dalhalla, a unique outdoor festival stage created in a disused limestone quarry. But it is opera that really brings out the best of Dalhalla: a magnificent natural backdrop with incredible acoustics means very little or no amplification is required. Where better for a passionate performance of Carmen or the oriental exoticism of Turandot?

Did you know? Dalhalla is situated in the area known as the Siljan Ring, formed when a meteorite collided with the Earth's surface during the Devonian period. It is the largest prehistoric impact crater in Europe, with a diameter of approximately 52 km.

BOTTOMLESS PIT

FALUN COPPER MINE

The rich, red soils of Falun have been a national resource for almost a millennium. Mining operations began here as early as the 10ᵗʰ Century, and by the 17ᵗʰ Century, the mine had become the foremost source of copper in Europe, and financial fuel to Sweden's rise as a great power.

When mining finally ceased in 1992, it was the end of an era. Thankfully, the site's UNESCO World Heritage status means the impressive story of 'The Great Copper Mountain' has now been preserved – for another millennium, perhaps.

Did you know? The typically red wooden houses you see all over Sweden are traditionally painted with *Faluröd*, a pigment made from iron oxides and other mineral residues from the copper mine in Falun.

CONNECTIVITY IS THE KEY

GÖTA CANAL

Born out of a desire to modernise Sweden and provide a more efficient cargo route, the Göta Canal is a great feat of 19th Century engineering, creating a continuous water way from Gothenburg in the west to Stockholm in the east.

These days, the 190 km canal between Mem and Sjötorp is one of Sweden's best loved tourist attractions. Cycle the distance down the towpath, luxuriate on a vintage steamship, or navigate the 58 locks in your own boat – the choice is yours!

Göta Canal goes with Baltzar von Platen, Thomas Telford, Motala Verkstad, Östra Götaland

THE BIG BLUE

LAKE VÄNERN

It comes in one size only: XXL. Covering an area of 5 655 km² and spanning three provinces, Lake Vänern is the biggest lake in Sweden – and the EU.

If you want to be at the heart of this watery expanse, head for Djurö, one of 30 small uninhabited islands on the lake. Located 11 km away from the mainland, it's more than a swim away though – you'll need your own boat to get there!

CINDERELLA DREAMS

LÄCKÖ

Gracing the shores of Lake Vänern at Kållandsö, Läckö Slott is one of the most fairytalesque of castles, bewitching visitors with its Baroque beauty.

It is thanks to the extensive construction work of Count Magnus Gabriel De la Gardie in the Mid-17th Century that the castle acquired its good looks – an aesthetic we still appreciate today.

ISLAND LIFE

SUNDSKÄR

Venture out to the extremities of the Stockholm archipelago and bask in the most serene of sunsets. Finding a secluded spot is not too difficult, as there are some 30 000 islands to choose from on this vast, fragmented stretch of coastline.

While many islands of the archipelago are barren and uninhabited, others, like Sundskär, have a long history of settlement. Sundskär may only be 1.5 km long but it has been populated since the 16th Century and sustained farming communities. A famous name or two may also have paid a visit: Gösta Bohman (an influential Swedish politician in the 1970s) had his summer house on the island.

Sundskär goes with…archipelago getaways, Baltic coast, simple summer idyll

GOING ROUND IN CIRCLES

SAXARFJÄRDEN

Now here's a rarity: a perfectly round island. This one has a little lighthouse, help-
ing vessels steer their course through Sax-
arfjärden. Also rare is the calm wrinkled
skin of these waters – a fickle change of
weather will give seafarers a rough ride.

51

BIG GUNS

VAXHOLM

Sweden's first line of defence begins in the archipelago, as clearly demonstrated by Vaxholm fortress, built in the early 17th Century. Vaxholm was important in defending Stockholm from the Danes in 1612 and from the Russians in 1719. As time passed, strategic defence moved out to the furthest reaches of Sweden's island territory.

A hop and a skip across the water from the fortress is the thriving town of Vaxholm, attracting summer visitors from Stockholm by the ferry load.

AYE AYE, CAPTAIN!

SANDHAMN

Sandhamn transforms itself from small, sleepy harbour to sailing mecca when it hosts the prestigious Round Gotland (ÅF offshore) race each July. The otherwise sparsely populated village brims over with hundreds of boats and thousands of visitors all summer.

Did you know? Popular Swedish crime writer, Viveca Sten has brought even more fame to the island with her Sandhamn Murder series.

SIMPLY SKIMMING THE SURFACE

NORR MÄLARSTRAND

Yes, when conditions are right, you can skate to work from one side of Stockholm to the other. But on a perfect day like this, let's not waste our efforts on a commute: with the sun in the sky and the Mälaren frozen to a mirror, it's time to glide beyond the city limits.

Did you know? *Vikingarännet* – the 'Viking Run' is an annual ice-skating event which was introduced in 1999. In some years, the ice is fantastic and it is possible to skate the whole distance (80km) between Uppsala and Stockholm. In recent years, poor ice has forced the organisers to cancel or cut short the race.

KNOCKING ON HEAVEN'S DOOR

SKOGSKYRKOGÅRDEN

Gentle undulating hills, elegant Functionalism and majestic pines make The Woodland Cemetery a very special final resting place. From its inception in the early 1900s, the idea was to create something different, a place where nature and architecture would blend into a harmonious whole.

Although the cemetery opened in 1920, construction would continue for another twenty years, with the completion of the iconic Woodland Crematorium and three chapels in the summer of 1940. Sadly, their famous architect, Gunnar Asplund, died just months later. He would be honoured with a place in his own cemetery, along with other Swedish greats including the actress Greta Garbo and choreographer Birgit Cullberg.

Skogskyrkogården goes with… Swedish Functionalism, Gunnar Asplund, Sigurd Lewerentz, UNESCO World Heritage Site

SUBTERRANEAN SOPHISTICATION

STOCKHOLM SUBWAY

On a drab winter's day in the city, a trip underground may prove more colourful. Over 90 of Stockholm's 100 subway stations have been decorated with art, embracing all manner of styles and materials, from mosaics and paintings to engravings and sculptures.

It's a historical journey too, charting artistic vision through the decades, from when the first stations were built in the 1950s to the newest ones, in the 1990s. With construction set to start on the brand new Yellow Line in 2018, 'the world's longest art exhibit' is likely to maintain its reputation!

Fun fact: Stations on the Blue Line are some of the most eye-catching, for example, Kungsträdgården, Rådhuset (pictured), Huvudsta and Tensta

A CAPITAL VIEW

SÖDER MÄLARSTRAND

A postcard perfect view across the water from Söder Mälarstrand (left) to Riddarholmen and City hall (right).

A ROCK FULL OF HISTORY

GOTLAND

As the sun gently melts into the horizon, what do you see? A lone hiker with the sea breeze in her hair, backpack weary after a long day? Or a tiny figure kneeling in the shale as he contemplates the shoreline?

The stark landscape of these neighbouring islands is food for the imagination – not least the coastline – with its weird and wonderful rauks or natural limestone pillars, eroded by the centuries. And what stories of old are buried in these silvery sands? If you dig deep enough, perhaps you will uncover an Arabic dirham. Great hoards of these silver coins have been discovered on Gotland, pointing to a time when the Vikings were trading in Germany, Russia and further South to the Caliphate along what is known as the Silver-Fur Road.

Gotland goes with…Ingmar Bergman, UNESCO World Heritage site, Hanseatic League, limestone quarries, wild ponies, summer holidays, medieval games

IN NOMINE PATRIS

VISBY, GOTLAND

Walk the cobbled streets of Visby and you could easily feel like you're walking straight into the 13th Century. Needless to say, the town thrives on its Hanseatic heritage and is a magnet for history buffs and medieval re-enactment fans alike. Here, the atmospheric ruins of Sankta Katarina church remind us of when being a Franciscan monk was all the rage.

CRIES AND WHISPERS

DIGERHUVUD, FÅRÖ

Drama is in the air…as always on Ingmar Bergman's island. The rugged, wild feel of Fårö is what first brought the film director here in 1960, on a location search for his film, *Through a Glass Darkly*. Fårö continued to inspire Bergman's creativity in subsequent films, and he soon made it his home.

Artistic talent is still nurtured on the island through the work of the Bergman Estate, and every summer, the Bergman festival attracts culture enthusiasts from around the globe.

BIRDS OF A FEATHER

STORA KARLSÖ

If Gotland and Fårö aren't wild enough for you, then the tiny island of Stora Karlsö surely is. The second oldest natural reserve in the world after Yellowstone in the US, Stora Karlsö is renowned for its bird life – particularly guillemots and razorbills, who favour the dramatic cliffs as their breeding ground.

Ornithologists will love a trip to the island at the end of June/beginning of July, when the little guillemot chicks jump from their cliff top abodes down to the shoreline to join their parents out at sea.

Did you know? Guillemot eggs are pear-shaped, minimising the risk of their rolling off the cliff edge.

THE WIND IN MY SAILS

JORDHAMN, ÖLAND

Despite its pencil-thin land mass, Öland has wide appeal. Around 500 km of coastline and over 50 bathing spots makes the island a beach lovers' paradise, and the bridge to Kalmar on the mainland gives happy campers easy access.

But why the windmill? The 'island of sun and winds' has a long history of successfully harnessing its natural resources in the pursuit of agriculture. There are no less than 350 windmills on Öland today, although historians suggest there were up to 2 000 windmills in the Mid-19th Century, at the height of pre-mechanisation.

Öland goes with... Solliden – the Swedish Royal Family's summer residence, Karlevi Rune stone, Borgholm castle, Stora Alvaret, biodiversity, UNESCO world heritage site

CHILLED TO THE BONE

ÖLAND

The nature of its geography and exposure to the elements makes Öland a harsh environment in winter. The vicious *Ölandsfåk*, a storm of strong winds, snow, ice and fog will force even the toughest islanders to confinement indoors.

WHAT LIES BENEATH

VÄDERÖARNA

Above water, these rocky island out-posts revel in rugged beauty but it is beneath the waves that their full glory is revealed. Divers delight in submerged hanging gardens teeming with starfish, anemones and prawns or venture to the depths for the real eye candy of living coral reefs.

Did you know? Väderöarna, along with the Koster islands to the North, lie in the most biologically diverse ocean area of Sweden and are part of the country's first marine national park.

CELEBRITY CHIC

FJÄLLBACKA

This charming seaside idyll has been a summer escape for the rich and famous since the early 20th Century – Ingrid Bergman even has a square named after her. And with Camilla Läckberg perpetuating its allure through the pages of her crime novels, there appears to be no end to the fascination with Fjällbacka.

Fjällbacka goes with… Ingrid Bergman, Camilla Läckberg, Tanum rock carvings, UNESCO World heritage site

MAKING WAVES

MARSTRAND

Sailing isn't always the best of spectator sports, but a trip to Marstrand during Match Cup Sweden may change your mind. With two identical yachts pitted against each other just 15 metres from the shore, the race is easy to follow from land, and why not climb up to the top of Carlsten fortress for a bird's eye view?

Did you know? Marstrand's reputation as a race venue is on the up. It now also hosts the World Championship finals of the World Match Racing Tour, seeing the winner take an amazing USD 1 million in prize money.

SHIPPING MAGNATE

PORT OF GOTHENBURG

The largest port in Scandinavia and still expanding, Gothenburg is the door to the world for Swedish industry. Its location gives it logistical superiority, with the three Nordic capitals of Oslo, Copenhagen and Stockholm all within a 500 km radius.

As Gothenburg's 400th anniversary in 2021 draws ever closer, the city is getting ready to celebrate, not by basking in maritime history, but by investing in the future, with plans for new residential districts and Sweden's biggest skyscraper underway.

Gothenburg goes with… Chalmers University of Technology, Michelin star restaurants, Volvo, Gothia Cup

CATCH OF THE DAY

FESKEKÔRKA

Gothenburg is famous for its seafood, and where better to buy it than in a 'fish church'?

The Gothically inspired market hall was futuristic at the time of its construction in 1874, with an interior entirely free from pillars. It is now one of Gothenburg's major cultural attractions, and still the best place in town to pick up fresh fish!

A SAILOR'S DITTY

VINGA FYR, GOTHENBURG ARCHIPELAGO

Go west young man, for the saltiest sea spray and an adventure into the great blue yonder!

The tiny island of Vinga is the furthest land area west of Gothenburg and home to Vinga fyr, a lighthouse with a touch of history. For this was the childhood home of Evert Taube, one of Sweden's most famous troubadours of the 20th Century. Little wonder his songs are filled with the love of sailing – his father was a ship's captain and the lighthouse keeper at Vinga from 1889-1905.

SHIVER ME TIMBERS

VARBERG

Anyone for an ice-cold skinny dip? The invigorating practice of bathing in sea water all year round has a long history in Sweden, as evidenced by the many elegant, late 19th Century *kallbadhus* or open-air bathing houses dotted around the country.

This one in Varberg was built in 1903, providing visitors with a salty swim in the Kattegatt. Ladies – don't be shy: there are separate bathing areas for men and women and you will be rewarded for your bravery with a relaxing sauna.

Varberg goes with… spa culture, west coast resort, UNESCO World Heritage site Grimeton radio station

PASTURES NEW

SMÅLAND

Contemplating this cosy countryside scene, it may be difficult to imagine hardship and suffering lurking in the shadows. But when Vilhelm Moberg began writing *Utvandrarna* (*The Emigrants*) in the late 1940s, memories of extreme poverty and famine were still fresh in the minds of many Swedes.

Moberg's epic quartet follows the trials and tribulations of a typical family from rural Småland in an era when around 1.5 million Swedes emigrated to the USA, in search of a better life. But what of Småland today? Well, time heals all wounds and now the whole region is a celebration of culture, with many visitors flocking here to enjoy famous attractions such as Astrid Lindgren's World and the Kingdom of Crystal!

Did you know? Älmhult in Småland is the birthplace of IKEA. You can now visit the museum 'IKEA through the Ages' to see how the furniture giant's designs have evolved over the decades!

THE LEAFY LOW-DOWN

SÖDERÅSEN NATIONAL PARK

Mile upon mile of beech forest is yours to roam at Söderåsen, perhaps best enjoyed while it displays the vibrant colours of autumn. With its dramatic ravines and undisturbed old growth, the atmosphere in this forest is truly special.

Did you know? Söderåsen is one of the largest expanses of uninterrupted protected deciduous forest in northern Europe.

KEEPING IT FRESH

MALMÖ LIVE

Funny how a city on the southern edge of Sweden can be so...edgy. Malmö has always been an architectural trend-setter, from commissioning Sweden's first high rise apartment block Kronprinsen in the 1960s to embracing re-development of the western harbour with its pièce de resistance Turning Torso in the 2000s.

Malmö Live concert hall and The Clarion hotel are two new additions, jazzing up the cityscape around the Central Station, while further afield at Hyllie, the massive Emporia shopping centre is just one of the area's latest architectural attractions.

Malmö goes with... visionary architecture, Öresund bridge, gateway to the continent

WEST SIDE STORY

VÄSTRA HAMNEN

Santiago Calatrava's landmark skyscraper symbolises a new era of modernity for the formerly downtrodden docklands of Västra Hamnen. Gracefully twisting 190.4 metres into the sky, Turning Torso is the tallest building in Scandinavia and one of the most elegant of residences in the trendy western harbour.

ON A ROLL

STAPELBÄDDSPARKEN, MALMÖ

As concrete jungles become more common than leafy ones, the modern explorer has to learn new tricks. In navigating this landscape, superb balance and agility take over from compasses and machetes. Glide to where you set your sights, and tackle obstacles in your path with a quick flip and a gravity-defying spin.

Stapelbäddsparken is one of four outdoor skate parks in Malmö. These, plus the 2 000 square metre indoor phenomenon, Bryggeriet Malmö Skatepark, make the city a world class skateboard destination.

Malmö goes with… urban street style, international atmosphere, music mecca, Zlatan

HARVEST OF PLENTY

KLÅGERUP

These golden fields are gold indeed to the farmers of Skåne who grow this important crop. Ninety per cent of all rapeseed from Sweden is used in the food industry; biodiesel is another area. But the cold pressed oil of the seeds is Skåne's pride and joy, and you'll see many farm shops selling their own organic rapeseed oil – liquid sunshine in a bottle.

Fun fact: Three kilos of rapeseed are needed to produce one litre of cold pressed oil.

ITSY BITSY BIKINI

SKANÖR-FALSTERBO

With fine white sand to rival that of the Caribbean, Skanör-Falsterbo should feature on any beach-bum's bucket list. Located as it is on the south-western tip of Sweden, the weather may be a little less Caribbean, but on any fine day in June-August expect to find plenty of sun-seekers and perhaps a skinny dipper or two!

MAGIC CIRCLE

ALES STENAR

Bathed in the twilight of a Midsummer's moon, this megalithic monument could be the spiritual twin of Stonehenge. But Ales stenar (Ale's stones), just east of Ystad in Skåne, is smaller and younger – a typical Scandinavian stone ship comprising 59 boulders, considered to be a Bronze Age burial ground.

Situated 32 metres above the sea with magnificent views of the coast, it's easy to see why the site was selected as a suitable resting place for the mighty men of old. And in common with Stonehenge, the solar alignment of the boulders gives the monument an ethereal appeal, even today.

Ales stenar goes with… Ancient burial ground, Ystad, Wallander

LAND OF THE STAR-GAZERS

VEN

Nestling in the Öresund strait between Denmark and Sweden is the small jewel of an island, Ven. Here, a favourable climate allows it to grow Europe's northernmost crops of Durum wheat, which is prized for pasta making. But pasta was probably not on Tycho Brahe's mind when he decided to build his castle on the island in the 16th Century. Instead, the talented scientist was seeking out the optimal location for an observatory, and Uraniborg on Ven soon became the leading astronomical research centre of its time.

PHOTOGRAPHS

LOCATION INDEX